FOOL IN ETERNITY
and
HE FELL IN THE CROWD

two plays by
Wadie M. Andrawis

American Literary Press, Inc.
Five Star Special Edition
Baltimore, Maryland

Fool In Eternity and He Fell In the Crowd

Library of Congress
Cataloging in Publication Data
ISBN 1-56167-597-0

Library of Congress Card Catalog Number:
99-091838

Published by

American Literary Press, Inc.
Five Star Special Edition
8019 Belair Road, Suite 10
Baltimore, Maryland 21236

Manufactured in the United States of America

A Fool In Eternity

Characters

Sam	Dr. of Cloning, in his forties
Janice	Sam's Wife
Brent	Sam's son
Sara	Sam's daughter
Mortician	
Monica	Sam's Girlfriend
Larry	Sam's Assistant
Grandfather	
Grandmother	
Angel 1 and 2	
Devil 1 and 2	
Jim	A sinner
Gigi	A sinner, Jim's Wife
Eddie	A sinner
Limo	A sinner
Amazing	A sinner

Act One

Scene 1

Scene: SAM, in his late forties, appears to be wealthy with a strong personality. The curtain opens. SAM sits in front of his computer, sipping on coffee. He appears preoccupied. His twelve-year-old son enters.

BRENT: *(excited, yells out)* Dad, did you see that?
SAM: What are you talking about?
BRENT: Your news is all over the Internet!
SAM: *(continues to work on his computer)* The whole world is on the Internet now.
BRENT: But, Dad, they're saying you're a world renowned physician and researcher in the field of cloning.

(SARA, his daughter aged 14 enters)

SARA: Of course he's the best. He cloned my Barbie doll when I was a little younger. When I was a little older, he cloned my dog, Pluto.
SAM: Well, I need to get going now.
BRENT: Why don't you come with us to Grandma and Grandpa's ranch this weekend?
SAM: You know I'm very busy. Go ahead and get ready because your mother should be here any time.
SARA: Dad, I'd like you to clone Jess.
SAM: Who is Jess?
BRENT: Jess is her boyfriend who she met over the Internet.
SAM: Why would you want to have him cloned?
SARA: So that I can take him with me when we go to the ranch.
SAM: Wow, is this tomorrow's generation?
SARA: Yes, Daddy, but why did you clone the plumber, the trash man, and the electrician?
SAM: So that we can save a few bucks.

SARA: You even cloned our family doctor.

SAM: You know these HMOs are terrible. You're just a number at their offices. Usually they have you wait for treatment until you die.

SARA: But, Dad, why did you clone yourself for Mom?

BRENT: Because he's always busy.

SAM: Yes. That way she won't be lonely when I am away.

SARA: I don't want to be lonely either.

SAM: Cloning's not an easy thing, off course. I can't just do it right now.

SARA: You know what, I've put that all into consideration, so that the cloning will be easy.

SAM: What do you mean?

SARA: I got an egg from him.

SAM: *(Baffled)* You got an egg from him?

BRENT: An egg, a real egg?

SARA: Yea.

SAM: *(Amazed)* An egg from a boyfriend??

BRENT: Does your boyfriend lay eggs?

SARA: Well, smarty, a rooster can't lay eggs.

SAM: *(Teasing her)* What's going to happen when you grow-up and get married? What are you doing to do with your husband?

SARA: Dad, you're talking a bunch of strange stuff.

SAM: *(Mocking seriousness)* I do believe your issue needs to be studied and researched further.

SARA: Studied and researched for what, Dad? *(She takes an egg out of her pocket)* Look, this is the egg, Dad. You want to get to work now?

(SAM takes a deep breath, and pets her on the shoulder, as he takes the egg from her)

BRENT: Why don't you make us an omelet?

SARA: This is a boiled egg.

SAM: *(Begins to peel the egg)* Now, I don't have to worry about you.

(JANICE *enters as* SAM *starts to eat the egg)*

SARA: *(Frightened)* Dad, you just ate Jess' egg. *(She starts to cry)*
JANICE: What's going on?
SARA: *(Angrily, crying)* I don't care. I need my Jess.
JANICE: What's that in your mouth? *(She looks to* SAM*)*
SARA: Dad just ate Jess.
SAM: *(Swallows the egg, and takes a couple of sips of milk)* I was just trying to conduct a new cloning experiment.
SARA: Dad, you're a liar, and you're going to hell.
BRENT: What do you mean by hell?
SARA: Adults know what that means. Mom, where is hell at? *(The bell rings)*
JANICE: Sara, please calm down and get the door.
BRENT: I got it.

(He runs ahead of his sister to open the door)

BRENT: *(Excitedly)* Grandma and Grandpa are here!
SAM: *(As the grandparents enter)* What a pleasant surprise!
GRANDPA: You must be very busy people. We never get to see you like before.
SAM: No, whenever we call you, the line is always busy. You must be surfing the web day and night.
SARA: *(Playfully)* Grandpa, are you dating some chick on the web?
JANICE: Don't be silly, Sara.
GRANDPA: *(to* SAM*)* Are you coming to the ranch to spend a few days with us, like you always have?
GRANDMA: I am sure Sam's too busy this time.
GRANDPA: The guy hasn't said a word yet.

SAM: *(Smiles)* My mother-in-law always understands me.

GRANDPA: Does that mean you're not coming?

SAM: Sorry, but I'm very busy with some research for the upcoming conference in England.

JANICE: *(Looking at her father)* He's always busy with his research, conferences, or cloning.

SARA: That's why Dad cloned himself for you, ha!

GRANDMA: He cloned himself.

JANICE: *(Hastily)* No, it's just one of his cloning experiments.

GRANDMA: I don't understand.

GRANDPA: Me either.

BRENT: Your generation is so behind, Grandpa!

SARA: You know Grandma! That's a great idea. Maybe, my Dad can clone Grandpa for you.

SAM: *(To JANICE)* Why don't you take Sara and get us some ice cream and something to drink?

SARA: Beer?

(JANICE and SARA leave)

GRANDPA: Today's generation is very hard to understand. I worry about them.

SAM: Our world is changing indeed. Science is advancing. Computers are taking over. And if you want to keep up, you have to ride the wave.

GRANDMA: I'm afraid this is the wave that will drown us.

BRENT: Grandma, now we have something called the Internet, genetic engineering, superior technology, NASA for space research—

GRANDMA: Lord, have mercy on us!

SAM: Don't forget we're in the 21st century.

GRANDPA: You're always working so hard, Sam. You really need some time off and our ranch is just the place to recuperate and renew your energy.

SAM: What can I do? This is out of my hands. Anyway, I'll get my vacation in a few days.

(JANICE and SARA return with the drinks)

JANICE: He's always like that, Mother. Whenever I ask him to go out like other couples, he says that he's busy. Sometimes, I feel like he's forgotten he's married and has kids who have rights, too.

GRANDPA: He works this hard for who?

GRANDMA: Let's get going and get ready to leave. Why don't we get your bags ready!

(GRANDMA exits with JANICE, SARA, and BRENT)

GRANDPA: Sam, I am truly proud of you.

SAM: Thanks.

GRANDPA: Sam, I want to ask you for a favor.

SAM: Sure, how can I help you?

GRANDPA: *(Whispering)* Would you be able to clone your mother-in-law?

SAM: My mother-in-law?

GRANDPA: But make her younger.

SAM: You mean a young woman?

GRANDPA: Yea, in her twenties.

SAM: But that would make her too young for you.

GRANDPA: Don't you worry Sam. Viagra is always handy.

(JANICE, GRANDMA, BRENT, and SARA enter)

GRANDPA: Well, why don't we talk about it when we get to the ranch?

GRANDMA: What is it you want to talk about?

GRANDPA: *(Devilishly)* Long live science, and its great

service for man. Now let's go.

(All leave the stage, except SAM. He sits down, and uses the phone)

SAM: Hello, hi Larry. Today.....yes,.....no.....don't worry. My wife and kids went to the ranch.......What? Do you have a surprise for me?........Oh, ...yes, I do remember her. And who doesn't know ?.....Don't you worry, you'll get your fair share....No, no Everything will be ready.....All night long. *(He hangs-up the phone, and looks at the wall clock)*

SAM: Wow, I have 5 hours till she gets here. I better take a nap now.

(He leans on the sofa and sleeps. Soft music plays. He starts dreaming. The phone rings, and he picks it up.)

SAM: Monica, are you out there? Come on up! That's fine. 15 minutes is fine. *(He hangs up the phone, and the doorbell rings)*

SAM: She's here already? *(He opens the door, and the mortician walks in and looks at SAM and SAM looks back at him)*

SAM: Can I help you?

MORTICIAN: Of course. I need your help. Where is he?

SAM: Who are you?

MORTICIAN: I have the most important job before the final exit.

SAM: You must be working for the IRS!

MORTICIAN: The IRS kills people, and leaves the everlasting frown on their faces. But I give the dead life, and I put an eternal smile on their faces.

SAM: What do you do?

MORTICIAN: My job is customer satisfaction.

SAM: Who are your customers?
MORTICIAN: The dead.
SAM: You mean you work at the mortuary?
MORTICIAN: You said it. Now, where is my customer?
SAM: You must have the wrong address.
MORTICIAN: Is this 3700 Main St.?
SAM: No, this is 3700 Overlook St. Maybe you need to
  check the address with your supervisor.
MORTICIAN: He's dead.
SAM: OK, now you get out of here!
MORTICIAN: Here's my business card. Your neighbor,
  your wife, any of your kids, even yourself, you can come
  to me, and we'll give you the best look and smile for
  your eternal rest.

*(The doorbell rings. SAM opens the door, and
MONICA, a pretty woman, walks in)*

MONICA: Hello Sam. I didn't know you had company.
MORTICIAN: I am the best company too. I promise I can
  give you a better smile when you are ready to go. I have
  a gift for you.
MONICA: Why me?
MORTICIAN: You seem like a lucky woman to me.
MONICA: What's the gift?
MORTICIAN: The best of fabrics—100% natural silk.
MONICA: Wow, that'd make a great dress.
MORTICIAN: You can buy the dress from any store. But
  my material you can't find anywhere.
MONICA: What are you talking about?
MORTICIAN: Pretty lady, I'm talking about the coffin.
SAM: Get out of here! *(The mortician leaves)*

(MONICA laughs)

MONICA: What a strange man? Who was he?

SAM: Wrong address.

MONICA: What's wrong? I don't want to see you with that frown on your face. You look silly like that.

SAM: This is very confusing. While I wait for pleasure and happiness, I end up getting a messenger of death.

(MONICA laughs out loud)

MONICA: Don't worry, he's gone. Now I am all yours.

(The music plays. She hands him a glass of liquor)

MONICA: Larry told me you were a genius.

SAM: Me?

MONICA: Yes, he told me you were successful in everything—in your work and research, in your home, with the people, and even in the elections and congress.

SAM: You must be Monica.

MONICA: *(Laughing)* You look a lot better when you smile. I'm going to give you the time of your life, more than any other Monica in the world.

SAM: That's what I am looking for.

MONICA: You wanna dance?

SAM: Sure, why not.

(She hands him a glass of wine and kisses him on his lips. JANICE walks in)

SAM: *(Confused)* Janice

MONICA: You got drunk that quickly? It's Monica, not Janice.

(JANICE comes in between them)

JANICE: And you're cheating on me in my own house. *(To* MONICA*)* I'm sorry I ruined your party.

MONICA: I guess I better go. *(She kisses* SAM *and walks out)*

JANICE: I wouldn't have found out had I not come back.

SAM: Don't be too upset. Let me explain.

JANICE: You don't have to say anything. I saw it all. If you really want to keep me now, you'll have to clone me. Because you know what—I'm leaving.

SAM: Cloning won't work, sweetheart. It won't be you.

JANICE: Liar.

SAM: What are you talking about? You need to listen to me. You don't believe in me any longer?

JANICE: After what I saw with my own eyes, and what I heard with my own ears, I can't believe you any more.

SAM: No, honey, you're wrong. You're being too rash.

JANICE: That's why I have to go.

SAM: Sweetheart, what are talking about. Where would you go?

JANICE: I'm going back to my parents. I need to look after myself, too.

SAM: Honey, don't be crazy.

JANICE: I'd be crazy if I ever lived with you another day. I've put up with this behavior for a long time. Sam, you've changed.

SAM: Who am I then? *(Struck with an idea)* This is a mistake. I am the cloned Sam. The real Sam went to England for the conference. He had to leave early.

JANICE: I know you're the real Sam because your cloned version is good for nothing.

SAM: *(Still pretending)* I thought you were satisfied with me, the cloned Sam.

JANICE: The cloned Sam is a big lie. You made it, but you didn't create it. And you actually believe your delusional science as reality.

SAM: *(Agitated)* No way.

JANICE: A man like you, what do you think you are? You're the devil. You were human when you were honest, sincere, when you knew true love and dedication. I loved your nobility. *(She pauses then continues bitterly)* Now, I hate you, I hate you, I hate you because you've killed that human voice inside you.

SAM: *(Collapses)* Please, I don't want to hear it. I don't want to hear it.

JANICE: I'll be quiet, but I am leaving—me and the kids. *(She runs off stage in rage. Music plays)*

SAM: *(Desperately)* Janice, Janice—(He looks around. He stutters to himself, stumbles around, grabs a drink of wine, and appears lost and confused)*

Stage darkens with song

Scene 2

Scene: SAM's *house.* SAM *and* LARRY *enter together.*

LARRY: I don't understand why you're so miserable. Take a look at yourself in the mirror!

SAM: *(Painfully)* For three long months, I haven't seen my wife and kids.

LARRY: *(He hands* SAM *a cigarette)* Everything will be all right.

SAM: I doubt it. Janice is wounded. Her pride is crushed. I'm dead sure she hates my guts. Who would blame her?

LARRY: Why don't you try to talk things over with her?

SAM: It's hard for man to confront his victim.

LARRY: Anyways, we'll find a way out of this.

SAM: What do you think we should do though?

LARRY: Let me think about it. But, I do have some good news for you.

SAM: Is there any good news left in this world?

LARRY: Of course—paradise, Monica's paradise.

SAM: Monica!

LARRY: Yes—Monica. That voluptuous cutie who brought you all this fortune.

SAM: Yeah. I've become a household mockery because of the media, I'm losing my wife. I'm under great pressure at work. What a fortune.

LARRY: I thought you guys had the time of your life together.

SAM: At the time, it felt great, but it turned out to be like a mirage.

LARRY: This girl is in love with you, she's crazy about you.

SAM: Larry, don't forget I'm a married man.

LARRY: Don't worry. There is no obligation. See you later.

(He leaves)

SAM: *(Talking to himself)* I'm the biggest loser on this earth, but I need to look after myself.

(Behind him, the cloned SAM *appears as the devil)*

DEVIL: That's awesome—whiskey, music, and a cigar.
SAM: Guess I should light it. *(Tries to light the cigar)*
DEVIL: *(Blows out* SAM's *flame before he lights his cigar)* This cigar is not for smoking, learn from the experts. This cigar costs 40 million dollars or more.
SAM: 40 million! How many homeless can be fed with that?
DEVIL: Think about it. Even the congressmen wanted to lynch him, but they couldn't, and all was forgotten.
SAM: Yeah. He took care of himself, and he enjoyed it.
DEVIL: And the whole world learned about it. But as long as everybody is doing well and the economy is booming, nobody cares.
SAM: It's a selfish world out there!
DEVIL: Even his wife stood by him. So learn from this expert. Don't curb your desire.

(They both laugh)

DEVIL: Your desire for Monica.

(SAM appears occupied, fills his glass with whisky, and starts to sip on it)

DEVIL: When Monica comes, your world will change. Her taste is like no other. Her eyes, her face, those lips, or that bod.(SAM *and the* DEVIL *laugh and scream out simultaneously)* Fire, fire, call the fire dept.

(The DEVIL *exits)*

SAM: *(Talking to himself, walks to the computer, and turns it on)* I should get some work done. Need to find out the latest on cloning research.*(A sound emitted by the computer starts)* Check system for failure.

SAM: *(Angrily)* There must be something wrong with the clones I am working on.

(He opens a room door, and the clones start shriveling)

SAM: *(Shocked)* My clones are dying. Oh my God, there're dying! Here is the trash man who suffocated from the odors. Ken, here is the plumber who drowned in his main. And Andy the carpenter died by the knock of his hammer. *(Hoping)* My clone is still alive. *(Appears troubled)* Sam, you appear so frazzled, why?

SAM CLONE: I am a human made by another human.

SAM: Then, you should have no deformities.

SAM CLONE: I'm very weak.

SAM: The implants I placed in you were perfect. You shouldn't be sick.

(CLONE shrinks and drops)

SAM: *(Seeking assistance from the* DOCTOR CLONE*)* Dr., Dr., help me!

DOCTOR CLONE: I am the one who needs help.

SAM: You're the one who's supposed to help me now.

DOCTOR CLONE: I can't move.

SAM: Doctor, I made you to heal my clones and help me out.

DOCTOR CLONE: *(His voice is frail)* I'm the one who needs the help.

SAM: These were my implants in you—the heart of a pig

and the brain of a chimp.

DOCTOR CLONE: That's why I can't be a doctor. *(His voice cracks)* Please help me, I'm dying, I'm dying. *(He drops to the floor)*

SAM: *(Laughs hysterically)* All is in vain. All my hard work has gone down the drain.All my clones are fake. But no. This can't happen! I cloned man and beast. I'm Sam who made man. And man has to live. *(He walks over to his computer)* Talk to me, you idiot! What's wrong?

COMPUTER: Pardon me sir. You are created, but not a creator.

SAM: Something is wrong with this program. I have to change it.

COMPUTER: *(Repeats)* You are created, but not a creator.

SAM: *(He pulls the plug)* Enough, I've had it!

(SAM sits down, fills his cup with wine, heads toward the door, and find a letter by the doorstep. He picks it up, and opens it while his son BRENT and daughter SARA appear in a panoramic scene).

BRENT: Dear Dad.

SARA: From the bottom of our hearts.

BRENT: We are so disappointed in you.

SARA: You've forgotten all about us.

BRENT: And for three months now, we've been feeling abandoned by you.

SARA: We've forgotten how to smile. We've even forgotten what you look like.

BRENT: And Mom—her life is in shambles.

SARA: Listen, Dad, we forgive you.

BRENT: But there's one condition. Our family has to reunite. *(BRENT and SARA in one voice)* Dad, we'll be waiting for you.

(The DEVIL *appears between the three of them)*

DEVIL: No, my son.
SAM: No, my son.
DEVIL: No, honey.
SAM: *(Talking to* SARA*)* No, honey.
DEVIL: You are still young. And you don't know what life is like. You need to have a blast. Pleasure comes from money and from Monica. That's the truth, and all of you out there are after this reality.
BRENT: Mom's life is in shambles.
SAM: Your mom is the reason. She loved you more than she loved me. I'm sorry, Brent. You're still young, and you don't understand that man looks after his own interests from birth. *(SAM looks where the devil was)* Yes, I'm still young, and I want to enjoy myself I have to live. Leave me alone, all of you. Leave me alone.*(SAM moves heavily in circles, and appears heavy laden, while accompanying music starts to play)* I've got to enjoy myself! I've got to enjoy myself! Monica! Monica! *(He laughs, and stumbles, and collapses at stage center)*

CURTAIN

Act Two

Scene 1

A funeral procession enters from the main entrance where the audience is seated. A coffin carrying the body of SAM is being paraded and SAM's family is following. They climb the stage as the curtain opens. The scene is a unique place where there is a large size scale placed in the center of the stage. SAM remains in the coffin. Heavenly music and sounds follow. Young angels enter and dance around him to wake him up before they exit. SAM appears bewildered as he starts to move around the stage staring at the atmosphere dazed.

SAM: Where am I? *(His voice echoes)* Where am I?

SAM: This is strange. *(His voice echoes)* This is strange.

SAM: Oh, I know what this is. This is the echo of my voice. Can a good Samaritan tell me where we are? *(He looks around, and claps his hands, and calls out)* Hey, you! Nobody wants to answer me! Maybe there aren't any good Samaritans out there.

(Two angels enter)

ANGELS: Peace be unto you.

SAM: (appears relieved) Yes, are you the good Samaritans?

ANGEL 1: We are angels.

ANGEL 2: We guard this place.

SAM: Hi guys.

(He tries to shake their hands, but the angels look at him without response)

SAM: You do look like angels. It's not fair that I be left here by myself.

(Both angels look at him surprised)

SAM: Why are you staring at me?

ANGEL 1: Don't waste our time.

ANGEL 2: Our mission is very specific.

SAM: Just tell me where we're at.

ANGEL 1: This is a waiting area

SAM: Waiting for what? Is this the INS?

ANGEL 1: You're waiting for eternity.

SAM: But, I don't want to go there.

ANGEL 2: This is not funny. We're not kidding.

SAM: What's going on here? What's happening to me?

ANGEL 1: This is the beginning of eternity.

SAM: Oh my God, is it that simple to transfer from world to world? It's hard to believe. To go from California to New York, it takes a long time. You're telling me I came here in an instant.

ANGEL 2: You were not expecting to leave your world.

SAM: I don't believe this.

ANGEL 1: Don't you realize that each man born on this earth, has to go to the other world?

SAM: Of course, I do.

ANGEL 2: That's exactly what happened to you.

SAM: But I'm still young.

ANGEL 1: Don't hide from reality. Death can't tell how old one is. It can't discriminate between rich and poor. It can't differentiate between ruler and ruled. And all of us have to go one day.

SAM: This is getting interesting. May I get coffee, and some donuts while I wait? And don't forget a cigarette too.

ANGEL 2: You need to understand life here is different from that of earth's. Here you gain spiritual immortality.

SAM: Like the ancient Egyptians?

ANGEL 1: Don't waste our time.

SAM: Could I at least check my email?

ANGEL 1: You have to know our mission is very clear.
SAM: What mission are you talking about?
ANGEL 2: You're now on trial.
SAM: Well then, I need to call my lawyer.
ANGEL 1: You won't find any of them. They already have been tried.
SAM: What are the charges?
ANGEL 2: Your sins.
SAM: Sins, do I look like a sinner?
ANGEL 1: Yes, the sins you've committed in your life.
SAM: I don't even know what sin means?
ANGEL 2: And you're lying too.
SAM: I'm telling the truth, and if you had any evidence, that would be a different matter. That would mean we'd have to go to trial, there would be appeals, and we might even go to the Supreme Court. That could take forever.
ANGEL 2: We have the evidence.
SAM: How can you store all the evidence against all people? Your mainframe must be overloaded.
(The angels exit)
SAM: *(Talking to himself)* Nobody understands, except for Monica and Larry.

(Both angels enter carrying a very lengthy printout)

ANGEL 1: On earth, his name was Sam Jacob. His age is 45 years old
ANGEL 2: On earth his profession was a cloning doctor.
SAM: That's right! And I can do you a favor.
ANGEL 1: His good deeds—

(He scrolls through the printout, and looks at the other angel who points to the printout)

ANGEL 2: He gave a homeless person a dry loaf of bread.

ANGEL 1: His traits include being selfish, being arrogant, and materialistic.

ANGEL 2: His apparent sins include attempting to create humans and giving in to his lust.

ANGEL 1: His hidden sins include all sins except for one thing.

ANGEL 2: Sins he never committed—only one: murder.

ANGEL 1: The judgment—hell for ever.

SAM: I did all this? That's me, but that's impossible. Are you serious about me going to hell? The real hell?

ANGEL 1: Definitely, this is the fate of every human who doesn't think about eternity.

SAM: *(Trembling)* Hell, no way, no, please do something, I don't want to go to hell. I wouldn't be able to stand it. Please, please.

ANGEL 2: That's impossible. Now it's too late. You had the chance when you were on earth.

SAM: I'm sorry, gentlemen. I need mercy and forgiveness. Heaven is full of mercy.

ANGEL 1: Don't even try it.

SAM: No I can't, heaven is merciful. Mercy, mercy.

ANGELS 1,2: Lord have mercy. *(They exit)*

SAM: *(Talks to self)* No, that's impossible—hell, no way. *(He gets quiet for a moment)* I can't believe all this is happening in an instant. *(He sits down)* How nice it would be to go back to earth, but that's impossible.

(A stranger enters blindfolded)

STRANGER: That's possible.

SAM: I never asked you. Who are you anyway?

STRANGER: I am a long time friend. I know you, but you don't know me.

SAM: But I've never met you.

STRANGER: We've met on many occasions before. We've met through those times of lust and pleasure. We're friends. Whenever you'd try to get away from me, I'd bring you back to make sure we'd be together forever.

SAM: Leave me alone. I have enough on my hands.

STRANGER: No friend, I won't leave you alone. I'm behind you all the way, and I'm gonna help you to go back to earth.

SAM: *(Hastily)* Ha, earth?

STRANGER: Yes, earth, life and pleasure.

SAM: Why, who are you?

STRANGER: I'm the one who can fulfill your wishes. Don't ask questions. Just follow my orders.

SAM: *(Thinks for a moment)* All right. What you're saying sounds fine.

STRANGER: Now, we're talking.

SAM: How much does it cost?

STRANGER: It's very expensive.

SAM: But I don't have a down payment, do I?

STRANGER: One always pays for my services at the end.

SAM: And those who don't pay?

STRANGER: So far, all those who chose me have always paid.

SAM: This is a hell of a business. All right. What next?

STRANGER: Now, let me tell you how you can go back to earth.

SAM: How?

STRANGER: There's only one way.

SAM: Tell me about it.

STRANGER: Go ahead and erase your sins.

SAM: Erase them? How can I do that?

STRANGER: *(The stranger hands him a magic wand)* With this magic wand, you can erase all the evidence.

SAM: *(In disbelief)* Come on! That stuff has to be backed up on their floppy.

STRANGER: No, no. There are too many people to be accounted for. The data can be downloaded only once.

SAM: Well, that makes sense.

STRANGER: That's right, if they have no evidence against you, they'll have to let you go.

SAM: *(Hesitating)* Yeah, but I don't know.

STRANGER: What about earth and all its pleasures? Don't be dumb. You get only one chance. *(Handing him the wand)* Here, take it.

SAM: No, no.

STRANGER: Here is your chance to go back to earth. The angels forgot your record of sins here. Now, it's your chance to erase them.

SAM: *(Talks to self)* Life on earth was full of pleasure. I've got to go back. *(He reaches for the magic wand and hesitantly starts to erase his record of sins)*

SAM: *(He yells out in joy)* My record is now clean. I've erased it. That's wonderful. You are a friend. *(He hurriedly goes toward the stranger and shouts)* A great friend.

(The stranger snaps the mask off his face, revealing an evil monster, who laughs hysterically. He walks away from SAM and disappears)

VOICE: Man, you are a fool. You were a fool on earth, and in eternity.

SAM: *(In fright, shocked)* Who's talking?

VOICE: You were fooled once again by the devil, you fool.

SAM: But the sins record was erased, and there is no evidence against me.

VOICE: Go ahead and take a look at your record of sins.

SAM: *(Looks over the record of sins, and nearly collapses)* The record hasn't changed, and they added one more sin.

VOICE: You fool—sins can't be erased unless you repent.

SAM: *(With sorrow in his voice)* Repentance!

(Two devils enter laughing)

SAM: What's so funny?
DEVIL 1: Because here you are, another fool.
SAM: You've cheated me, you lied to me.
DEVIL 2: You also tried to cheat in your eternal judgment.
SAM: I thought you were going to help me out.
DEVIL 1: Since when does the devil help man?
DEVIL 2: Do you think you're that smart?
DEVIL 1: We work very hard to recruit our victims. Some take more work than others.
DEVIL 2: We never waste time. We work year round, 24 hours a day. No time off, whatsoever.
DEVIL 1: Not even Labor Day, Christmas, the 4th of July, or even Thanksgiving.
SAM: Would you leave me alone?

(Both devils laugh at him)

SAM: Why do you keep on laughing all the time? What's so funny?
DEVIL 2: You. Because you're so foolish.
DEVIL 1: Now, it's time to come along with us.
SAM: No, I'm not going anywhere.
DEVIL 2: But this was your choice.
DEVIL 1: You're the one who chose hell.
SAM: I'm not going to hell—you're liars, cheaters, liars, cheaters.
DEVIL 2: You just found out. It's too late my friend.
SAM: Please, leave me alone. I need mercy.
DEVIL 1: Mercy? What is mercy?
SAM: You're damned.
DEVIL 2: And you're stupid because you chose our way.
DEVIL 1: You had so much pleasure on earth.

DEVIL 2: And we drowned you in your greed.

SAM: What would I have gotten if I gained the whole world?

DEVIL 1: You had so much influence and power, bank deposits, bonds, stocks, and all kinds of beautiful women.

DEVIL 2: Many people suffered from hunger and you wasted so much around you, and many couldn't even afford medicine and you owned and operated hospital chains.

SAM: All vanished over night. All evaporated like steam. All is in vain, all is in vain.

DEVIL 1: You were always in the lime light, and many revered you.

SAM: And now I'm despicable, I'm the scum of the earth. I'm lost forever.

(He collapses and moans, while the devils dance around him)

DEVIL 2: And now it's time to go.

SAM: Go where?

DEVIL 1: To the abyss.

DEVIL 2: And then on to hell.

DEVIL 1,2: Hell forever and ever.

SAM: (hysterically) I'm a fool, fool, fool.

(SAM is carried by the devils with music playing while he screams and wallows)

STAGE DARKENS

Scene 2

Scene: The abyss full of sharp edged rocks forming a seating arrangement, and in the middle, a very sharp gigantic rock used as the seat of confessions. Three men and a woman are circulating around the seat of confessions agonizing and wailing in response to the punishment being delivered to them.

EDDIE: This devil is disrespectful. I'm Eddie. Why are they grabbing me by the balls?

JIM: I doubt they found anything there.

EDDIE: I'm Eddie, the governor of Lalaland. They grab my balls! Where's my power and influence? Where are the secret service agents? Where are the machine guns? And where is the whip?

DEVIL 1: *(Always mocking)* So, you are Sir Eddie, the man of unlimited power and influence?

EDDIE: *(Proudly)* You said it.

DEVIL 2: We're sorry for your humiliation. *(Kicks him in the butt, laughing)*

EDDIE: Does the news of ball gabbing and butt kicking elicit all this laughter? I'm the governor of Lalaland. Where are the secret service agents? Where are the machine guns? Where is the whip?

DEVIL 1: You are Sir Eddie, who humiliated people with his power?

EDDIE: (proudly) You said it.

DEVIL 2: We are proud of you, Senor Eddie. And this is for you. *(He kicks him)*

AMAZING: *(A dumb young man)* Are you Sir Eddie?

EDDIE: Of course.

AMAZING: You should've been called Mr. Butt.

GIGI: I feel sorry for you.

EDDIE: Why should my balls get grabbed? Why should I

be kicked on the butt? Why am I being called Sir Butt? Why do you feel sorry for me? I'm Eddie, the governor of Lalaland.

LIMO: The more you say Sir Eddie, the more they'll kick your butt.

EDDIE: Your voice sounds kind of familiar to me.

LIMO: The same here.

EDDIE: Maybe we do know each other.

LIMO: It's possible. I've dealt with characters like you before.

JIM: What's going on here? Seems like everybody knows everybody here.

EDDIE: Do you know me?

JIM: I'm not talking to you, Mr. Butt. I'm talking about my lady.

EDDIE: *(Pointing to GIGI)* Is this your wife?

JIM: She was. Do you wanna take her place?

EDDIE: That's my limit. I can't take it anymore. I'm Sir Eddie, the governor of Lalaland. I ruled with an iron fist, and whoever got in my way, my agents took care of them. Some never came back.

GIGI: Be quiet, or they'll kick your butt again.

EDDIE: I'm Senor Eddie.

LIMO: Aha, now I recognize you.

EDDIE: And now I remember you.

LIMO: You were—

EDDIE: *(Interrupting)* And you supplied me with arms.

LIMO: Yea, you were my customer.

AMAZING: Do you own a barber shop?

JIM: My gosh, hell is heating up.

GIGI: I feel the fire coming closer.

JIM: You're always on fire.

GIGI: You're the one who starts it.

JIM: And you're the one who never knows what's going on.

GIGI: Me, or you Jim? You're very arrogant, thinking you're always smarter while you don't know your name from a hole in the ground. You're the one behind the loss of our family and the kids.

AMAZING: What's going on here? I feel like I'm being disrespected.

LIMO: Actually, you're the only one we don't know.

AMAZING: I'm Mr. Amazing. Unlucky to be with you forever.

EDDIE: I'm Sir Eddie, the all powerful here. Am I to live with you? You?

AMAZING: Yes, Mr. Butt. And you haven't seen nothing yet.

LIMO: We're gonna stay up all night at hell.

AMAZING: But Mom told me to go to bed early every night.

LIMO: This is a sleepless land. But we're gonna eat plenty, too.

JIM: Why don't you get me a shank of lamb?

GIGI: I'd like to order steak, medium rare.

LIMO: The menu here may be slightly different—breakfast will be pure fire, lunch will be fire of barbecue, and dinner is eternal fire.

GIGI: You mean, that's it? We'll be staying in this inferno for good?

LIMO: I wish. I hear this is nothing compared to hell.

GIGI: Jim, you're the culprit. It was the worst day of my life, the day I met you. I lost life and eternity, and I lost my youth as well.

JIM: Shut up, nobody asked you to talk.

GIGI: That's my destiny, and I can't do anything about it.

AMAZING: You look like a catastrophe waiting to happen. You deserve to be here.

GIGI: You dummy. *(She cries)* It's because I'm the only woman here, and there's no one to turn to.

JIM: That's OK Gigi, don't cry now. You know you brought all this upon yourself. We don't need to argue all the time because you can count on us being here for a long time to come.

EDDIE: *(Disgustedly)* Oh my God, I can't stand this woman. I feel like taking off.

LIMO: Where do you wanna go? To another inferno? This is it, buddy!

EDDIE: You mean no more option to buy or lease?

AMAZING: This is not a zoo, Senor Butt.

EDDIE: Don't call me Senor Butt! I'm Mr. Eddie.

GIGI: Forget what you were all about.

EDDIE: What do mean forget?

JIM: You'll get kicked on your butt, until you forget Sir Eddie and accept Mr. Butt as your new title.

LIMO: *(To EDDIE)* I feel sorry for you because you still live in the past. Here we're all equal, powerless, and destined to perish.

EDDIE: Yes. I feel I've lost it all. Where are my secret service agents? Where are the machine guns? Where is my whip?

AMAZING: Your secret service agents are all in hell now, and that whip you're talking about, maybe you can shove it up your ass.

JIM: And the guns, you can find them with the terrorists.

LIMO: Tell me Eddie, how were things recently?

EDDIE: I don't want to talk about it.

AMAZING: Kicks in the butt didn't kill you, did they?

EDDIE: My chief agent betrayed me, and threw me out in a coup, and finally put me me in jail. Two days later, the new chief agent threw out my ex-chief agent and jailed him with me.

GIGI: Did your wife visit you? Did she bring you food, doughnuts, pizza and hamburgers. Did you have spousal rights?

JIM: Hopefully, you didn't lose your virginity.

LIMO: You must have gotten executed, all of you.

EDDIE: The new chief didn't have enough time because the people revolted and arrested him, and the three of us were jailed.

LIMO: How come you weren't sentenced to death?

EDDIE: Jail was worse than death.

LIMO: Of course, that's a fair end.

EDDIE: Limo, you were a lot smarter than me. You lived and died strong and rich.

LIMO: And how did all that help me?

EDDIE: You deserve this, too.

AMAZING: *(To* LIMO*)* Now show your dirty laundry.

EDDIE: Limo, you sold me everything—propaganda, arms. You even purposely caused more turmoil to make more money off it.

JIM: Did Mr. Limo really deal in arms?

EDDIE: His arms destroyed lives. Wars erupted, and he watched people and children die. He didn't care. All he cared about was the almighty dollar.

LIMO: You know Eddie, you talk like you were innocent. You were the dumbest person around.

GIGI: This, I do believe. He lost his balls, and got kicked in his butt.

LIMO: Do you know what he used to do?

JIM: Did he buy the Brooklyn Bridge?

LIMO: Through his reign, he abused his authority. He deprived people of their liberties, and he chained their minds.

EDDIE: I was concerned about them.

GIGI: Is that a good reason to kill their freedom?

LIMO: You tried to protect yourself from the people, so you spied on them, and you placed listening devices all over the country fearing people would ask for their freedoms.

EDDIE: I wanted to secure the country.

LIMO: Security comes naturally with freedom.

EDDIE: Freedom means chaos.

LIMO: That's freedom without the rule of law.

GIGI: You were a dictator.

LIMO: Dictatorship is the rule of a single man supported by the police state. A police state has no room for opposition, and nobody can object or voice a thought.

AMAZING: Ever since he came here, we kicked his butt, and he couldn't do anything about it.

LIMO: It's because he's powerless over here. Now, all of us are in the same boat.

JIM: *(Talking to Gigi)* You brought this upon us.

GIGI: I'm innocent, Jimmy. You're the one who put us in this predicament.

JIM: What about your loose life?

GIGI: Because you were blind, you suspected everything, even yourself.

JIM: It's your behavior that made me think all these things. You were an ice-cold woman who never fulfilled my desires.

GIGI: How did you want me to feel romantic? All you wanted was to jump in bed.

AMAZING: This is confusing. Did you talk or make love?

GIGI: When I'd ask him to go out for a walk with the dog for 30 minutes away from his pager, the Internet, or a cell phone, he'd refuse.

JIM: Your dog was a stupid dog. He'd always pee on the neighbor's lawn. And he'd leave his famous mark all over town.

GIGI: You were always busy.

JIM: I was busy supporting our family to give all of us the comforts of life.

GIGI: Yes, you bought us all that we needed, but you never filled our home with the kind of love we so badly needed.

LIMO: That's life my friends: You live poor but fulfilled or you live rich and needy.

AMAZING: How many TV sets did you own?

GIGI: Just three of them.

LIMO: So you ended up with a set for you to watch your soap operas, a set for Jim to watch the adult channels, and a third set for the Jerry Springer show.

JIM: What mattered was that Gigi was happy.

GIGI: What about the kids?

JIM: Don't. I don't wanna remember.

EDDIE: What happened to the kids? Were they arrested or something?

JIM: It was hellish. My 16-year-old son, Todd—I saw his picture on national TV.

AMAZING: Was he discovered by a producer or something?

JIM: It was a horrific day. We thought he'd go to get an education, but that day, he shot a classmate and killed him. He then turned the gun on himself and fired, killing himself in the middle of the classroom.

AMAZING: That's sad, very sad.

JIM: And my other son, Richard, who is 20, got on drugs while in elementary school. At age 12, he quit school to be in a gang. He robbed, raped, and murdered with no conscience. Because he danced with the devil, he was shot by some gang member, and was destined to an evil life.

GIGI: Don't talk like you weren't to blame. You failed them as a father.

JIM: Oh yea, what about when I was disciplining Todd? You forgot the child abuse charges filed against me?

GIGI: You never disciplined him, you punished him, and by then it was too late.

LIMO: Both of you are to blame. You both lived self-centered lives, and the children were the victims.

JIM: Please, don't remind me. This hurts.

GIGI: Me too.

LIMO: All those who erred will have eternal fire that won't be put out. And a sword to punish them, but not kill them.

GIGI: Yes, all of us are paying the price, the price of sin. The price is too great, and we can't afford it. We can't withstand it.

AMAZING: Talk about affording, I've never owned anything.

LIMO: I'm afraid none of us can afford this price.

JIM: Whenever I remember the face of my daughter Sally, my heart gets filled with pain.

AMAZING: Was her face that painful?

JIM: No, the truth is that she got pregnant at age 17, and she dropped out of school after having the baby, and ended up being a call girl serving many lustful souls out there.

LIMO: You are both responsible for what happened to your children. You both looked after yourselves. Your children never found love and affection. Nobody showed them wrong from right.

AMAZING: You're right.

JIM: That's enough, I've had it. Something inside me is very painful. I wanna die.

LIMO: We all have it inside us.

GIGI: I'm hurting inside as well.

EDDIE: My pain is so great.

AMAZING: What the hell are you talking about?

LIMO: This thing you're all talking about, is the conscience. *(They all tremble and speak in one voice)* Conscience!

LIMO: Yes, conscience. All those who are here have killed their conscience on earth, so they're receiving their rightful punishment.

AMAZING: And how did he come to life again?

LIMO: He came to life after our earthly death, to dwell inside us in eternity. He'll hurt us, he'll take revenge, and the pain will be forever and ever.

JIM: Yes, I can't stand the pain. I'm in severe pain. I can't stand it, but if I could stand it, for how long will this go on?

EDDIE: No. The voices of those I jailed are screaming inside me, calling me unjust. I'm suffering. Silence these voices, silence them.

LIMO: And that's just the beginning of the non-ending pain.

JIM: Does that mean forever?

GIGI: That's just too bad. We lost our lives and our eternity.

EDDIE: You have the right to scream and wail. Gone is my power and authority. Gone are the machine guns. Gone is the whip, and gone is Lalaland.

AMAZING: You are all miserable people. I better get out of here to see the other side.

(He exits)

DEVIL: (Offstage) May the gates of purgatory open for another sinner.

(Scary music plays as SAM *enters, distracted, scared, and with eyes unfocused)*

GIGI: Welcome Mr. Sam.

SAM: *(Surprised)* Do you know me?

JIM: It seems all whom you know are women.

SAM: She called me by name.

EDDIE: All of us here know you.

SAM: But I never met you.

LIMO: It's because you're a famous man.

SAM: But my fame has led to my demise.

JIM: We're all friends.

LIMO: All gets uncovered here.

SAM: So, you all know the story of my reality.

LIMO: Here, all is uncovered and nobody can deny the truth.
GIGI: If I were your wife, I'd have made you a miserable
    person.
SAM: Who are you?
JIM: We're sinners.
EDDIE: We're evil ones.
LIMO: Miserable, dumb, and you're one of us.
SAM: Where are we?
JIM: This is a festival.
SAM: What festival?
LIMO: The festival of fireworks.
SAM: What's this gate?
EDDIE: Ever since you walked in here, you've been
    questioning us like the FBI.
GIGI: Let him ask all he wants. Talk is cheap.
EDDIE: Don't give him the wrong impression, Gigi.
    Welcome to our club.
LIMO: This is the gate of hell.

*(The devils enter in a dramatic procession to the sounds
of trumpets, and all tremble)*

DEVIL MASTER: My evil counterparts, you need to know
    that heaven kicked you out because you lived according
    to our ways, and you gave yourselves to us. You have
    fallen and could not liberate yourselves from the bonds
    of our chains. We are not gonna abandon you without
    refuge. I'd like to personally welcome you to hell, where
    you'll be with us for eternity. This is our right, and it's
    also yours. You will be honored to know, I'm the master
    devil. In hell there will many people, and more will
    come—millions and billions, and I'm the master of all
    hell.

(Laughter erupts with all the devils)

DEVIL MASTER: *(In an authoritative voice)* Let these gates of hell open, wide open.
DEVIL MASTER: Open to all the sinners, and the evil ones.

(The gates of hell open as billows of fire rumble accompanied by screams, moans, and sounds of wailing. All cry out. As they line up behind each other, an unseen force violently pulls them in)

ALL: No, no, no.
SAM: *(Frightened)* No way, leave me. I see awful, scary things. I hear the screams, the wailing is unbearable, and I can't take it. I can't live in this pain forever. No, no way. Let the earth swallow me. Let the mountains cover me and hide me. Let the rivers drown me. Woe to me, woe to me, woe to me.

(Music plays)

ALL: Hell, hell hell.

CURTAIN

HE FELL IN THE CROWD

Characters

Dr.Goodman	Psychologist, in his early forties
Karen	Goodman's wife, thirties
Christine	Their daughter, teenager
Michael	Their son, teenager
Nancy	Karen's friend, thirties
Joe	Dr. Goodman's patient, forties
Nurse	
Vagabond	

Act One

Scene 1

As the audience awaits the raising of the curtain, a voice says: "Ladies and gentlemen. We would want to direct your attention to the following. Tonight, you will have the option to select the solution to your psychological dilemma. If any of you has lost hope, tonight you will conquer your suffering. If betrayed by a friend, you will be restored. If tormented by your egoist brother, you will be taught to be forgiving. Ladies and gentlemen. Tonight, if you are chased by fear, you will find courage. Justice will vanquish oppression. Life will be renewed for whomever desires it. My dear viewer, you are about to meet the world-renown psychologist, DR. GOODMAN. Immediately after his press conference, he will be available to you. Discuss your problems with him in an open and shameless manner." Song announcing the arrival of DR. GOODMAN plays.

DR. GOODMAN walks on stage. A dapper gentleman in his early forties, dripping with energy and liveliness. He is carrying the Ten Commandments. Each commandment is on a separate paper. He is addressing the audience in a personal caring fashion. "What's the matter?" he asks. "What's hurting you?" he inquires. He hands a commandment to a member of the audience and moves on to another. After passing out all the papers, he stands near the front row. A beautiful woman, KAREN, stands, takes him by the hand, and faces the audience.

KAREN: *(Totally elated)* Look at your adoring fans, my darling.

DR. GOODMAN: *(He steps on stage with KAREN)* They are expecting hope.

KAREN: Does that mean more profit for us?

DR. GOODMAN: My work means more than money to

me.

KAREN: Don't forget darling that you worked all day.

DR. GOODMAN: Yes, but only to alleviate man's sufferings.

The Curtain Opens

The Scene: DR. GOODMAN's *living room, cozy and loving. Their wedding portrait prominently displayed upon the wall.*

KAREN: *(Pours a glass of wine and hands it to her husband)* It's OK to alleviate people's sufferings. But, they must pay for it; otherwise, we'll be in the poorhouse.

DR. GOODMAN: *(Takes off his coat, tosses it on the chair. KAREN picks it up and hangs it. He undoes his tie)* People are in need of someone to listen to their concerns.

KAREN: *(Coldly)* But they are sick, and you are treating them.

DR. GOODMAN: They are hurting, really.

KAREN: But you can't cure them all.

DR. GOODMAN: Why not talk about something else?

KAREN: What do you think about the wife who has an extra marital affair?

DR. GOODMAN: Poor fellow, he was deceived. Life deceived him. There is no friendship here, only an arrangement that is mutually beneficial.

KAREN: I can't believe what happened today.

DR. GOODMAN: What happened?

KAREN: A son asked his father for his inheritance.

DR. GOODMAN: Is he misguided?

KAREN: *(She hands her husband a glass of wine)* I sometimes feel for mankind.

Dr. GOODMAN: That son is a victim.

KAREN: *(She reaches for the television remote control)*

Let's watch this film.

DR. GOODMAN: Good idea.

KAREN: It's an excellent movie.

DR. GOODMAN: I agree.

KAREN: I think it is going to win a lot of Oscars.

DR. GOODMAN: For sure.

KAREN: You must be hungry.

DR. GOODMAN: That I am.

KAREN: Supper will be ready in minutes.

DR. GOODMAN: I'll change my clothes.

KAREN: Let's do it together.

DR. GOODMAN: Great idea. *(He takes her by the hand, into the bedroom. Later, they come out, giggling. KAREN sets the table, and they sit to eat)*

DR. GOODMAN: You are the best cook in the world.

KAREN: And you are the best husband in the world.

DR. GOODMAN: Did you choose a name for the baby?

KAREN: No. You choose first.

DR. GOODMAN: But you are the mother.

KAREN: And you are the father.

DR. GOODMAN: But you are the one carrying it.

KAREN: And you are the one that made it.

DR. GOODMAN: Let's flip for it.

KAREN: OK. *(Gets a coin)* You call it.

DR. GOODMAN: You call it first.

KAREN: All right, you are heads. I am tails.

(KAREN makes the toss, and she wins)

DR. GOODMAN: You always win that way.

KAREN: The baby's name shall be Michael.

DR. GOODMAN: I agree.

KAREN: Next time, when we have a girl, you will choose the name.

DR. GOODMAN: Okay.

KAREN: Which name will you choose?
DR. GOODMAN: Christine.
KAREN: I agree.

(They laugh. Music plays. KAREN hands him his glass of wine)

DR. GOODMAN: You make me so happy; especially tonight.
KAREN: I am happy being here with you.
DR. GOODMAN: Let's dance. Want to?
KAREN: Like every night? *(She reaches for his hand, and pulls him toward her, seductively)*
DR. GOODMAN: *(Gets closer)* You are beautiful.
KAREN: Do you love me?
DR. GOODMAN: *(They are now dancing)* Naturally, I love you. You are my life.
KAREN: Why do you love me?
DR. GOODMAN: You are intoxication, my elation, my wife, and my true happiness. I see nothing but beauty in you. *(He kisses her)* Do you love me as much as I love you?
KAREN: I know you love me. I am all yours.
DR. GOODMAN: I am also all yours.
KAREN: Then let's turn off the lights and be one with each other.
DR. GOODMAN: Your wish is my command.

(The lights dim. Music softly plays. Whispers, giggles, and laughter. The lights softly come back on. It is now two a.m. A baby crys)

KAREN: Goodman, please wake up.
GOODMAN: Why?
KAREN: Can't you hear Michael crying?

GOODMAN: Why is he crying?

KAREN: Maybe he's hungry.

GOODMAN: *(Moving slowly, still halfway asleep)* I can't stand this crying. I can't stand his hurt. Where is his feeding bottle?

KAREN: Maybe in his room.

GOODMAN: *(He enters the baby's room)* He is still crying.

KAREN: He maybe needs a diaper change.

GOODMAN: Where is the diaper bag?

KAREN: You woke me up for no reason.

GOODMAN: He is really hurting, my dear.

KAREN: Yes, I can hear his crying.

GOODMAN: Then, get up, and do your duty.

KAREN: *(Coldly)* I am really tired. Please do not disturb me. You know what to do.

(The baby continues to cry)

GOODMAN: I changed his diaper, and he is still crying.

KAREN: Pick him up, and shake him a bit.

(DR. GOODMAN carries the child on stage, singing and talking gaga googoo to his baby. He looks at the baby tenderly)

GOODMAN: I'll hurt to spare you the hurt. I'll stay up late, so you can sleep. I'll tire, so you can rest. I'll wipe your tears, day or night, and at any other time.

(The baby quiets down. KAREN awakens, and meets her husband on stage)

KAREN: Thank you, my dear. I tried to make him stop crying, but I couldn't.

GOODMAN: *(He tenderly hands her the child)* Take him.

Give him the real food from your breast. Make him fill your heart. Shield him in your bosom, because he is our child, our beautiful child.

(GOODMAN and KAREN sing to the baby in ecstasy. The stage lights dim and out)

Scene 2

The Scene: The Goodman's living room. KAREN *enters.*

KAREN: *(In a loud and exasperated voice)* Michael, Michael!

   (CHRISTINE enters. She appears to be about nineteen years of age)

CHRISTINE: It's no use, Mother, he's not answering.
KAREN: *(Snapping)* What's he doing now?
CHRISTINE: He's busy.
KAREN: Doing what? Preparing his things?
CHRISTINE: *(Helping prepare supper)* Yes, nothing seems to be more important.
KAREN: *(Setting the table)* You're right.
CHRISTINE: You know, Mother, that Kayla is the most important thing in your son's life.
KAREN: He's free to choose. *(Upset)* But he must do it in a hurry.
CHRISTINE: It's hard to know what they are talking about, especially when they are on the Internet.
KAREN: I'm tired of the computer and the Internet.
CHRISTINE: The world can't do without them.
KAREN: *(Worried)* His bag isn't ready yet?
CHRISTINE: *(Appeasing KAREN)* He should be done very soon.
KAREN: What about your bag? Is it ready?
CHRISTINE: You know me. I'm always ready on time.
KAREN: I hope you didn't forget anything.
CHRISTINE: No. But—
KAREN: *(Interrupting)* But what?
CHRISTINE: I hate to leave before my father gets home.
KAREN: Aren't you waiting for Mark?

CHRISTINE: I called him on his car phone. He's on the way.
KAREN: Then let's hurry, and get supper ready.
CHRISTINE: Are we going to eat without Dad?
KAREN: He'll have to eat alone, I guess.
CHRISTINE: You're right. I don't want to be late.

(They finish preparing the table, MICHAEL enters. He is in his twenties)

KAREN: Food seems the only thing to pull you away from the computer.
MICHAEL: You know, Mother, your food is so good, it pulls me away from anything.
KAREN: Are you going to eat first or finish packing?
MICHAEL: Eat, for sure.
KAREN: You'd better hurry, if you don't want to miss your plane.
MICHAEL: *(Eating)* I'll eat in five minutes and finish packing in five minutes.
CHRISTINE: And you're gonna get a speeding ticket if you try to get to the airport in five minutes.
MICHAEL: It doesn't matter. I don't care.
CHRISTINE: Your car insurance will go up again.
MICHAEL: My father will pay it.
CHRISTINE: You're so spoiled.
MICHAEL: And you're jealous.
KAREN: How's your food?
MICHAEL: Your food is always appetizing.
KAREN: What would you do without me?
CHRISTINE: Send him the recipe.
MICHAEL: Great. Send it to my Email address.
KAREN: You're gonna be late. Clear the table while I take a shower.

(KAREN exits)

MICHAEL: *(Heading toward his room)* I heard what Mom said.

CHRISTINE: As usual, you're gonna help clear the table.

MICHAEL: You're my favorite sister

CHRISTINE: *(She begins gathering up the dinner plates)* You're gonna have problems when you go out on your own.

MICHAEL: *(Answering her from his room)* No, no, I solve problems.

CHRISTINE: Who's going to fix your meals?

MICHAEL: Don't you worry about that. My friend is an excellent cook.

CHRISTINE: *(Packing leftovers into bags to be put in the refrigerator)* Are you sure about that?

MICHAEL: *(Leaving his room, luggage in hand)* I think jealousy has gotten the best of you.

CHRISTINE: Me?

MICHAEL: *(Putting his bag down)* Naturally.

CHRISTINE: You don't know how talented I am.

MICHAEL: *(Stuffing his bag with clothes)* At least my stomach won't hurt.

CHRISTINE: If it does, let Kayla take care of it.

MICHAEL: *(Pulls out KAYLA's picture from his wallet. He puts it close to his sister's face to incite her even more)* Look how pretty she is, huh!?

CHRISTINE: What a nose on her. Looks like a corn cob.

MICHAEL: It is at least smaller than yours.

CHRISTINE: Have you kissed those big thick lips?

MICHAEL: *(Kissing the picture)* Can't get enough of those lips.

CHRISTINE: *(She snatches the picture from his hand, looks closely at it)* Those eyes they look so dumb. She looks so unintelligent.

MICHAEL: Don't forget she's going to medical school at Oxford, my dear.

CHRISTINE: And you don't forget that I'm going to graduate from Harvard.

MICHAEL: *(Mocking)* As a lawyer?

CHRISTINE: Remember, I made you a bet that someday I will be become a Supreme Court Judge.

MICHAEL: And I will become a member of Congress.

CHRISTINE: Another scandal for the politicians.

MICHAEL: On the contrary, I will be a powerful advocate for true democracy.

CHRISTINE: If left to you, you will turn freedom into chaos.

MICHAEL: As usual, you talk and talk. But I must bow out of the fight and get ready to go.

CHRISTINE: Same here. I must get ready.

MICHAEL: You are always imitating and following me. Let's see who gets ready first.

(They exit, as if they are going to different bathrooms. The phone rings. KAREN enters the stage, hair dryer in hand, calling for her children)

KAREN: Michael! Christine! Will someone answer this phone?! *(She stops the hair dryer, picks up the phone)* Hello. Hi, Nancy, sure I am out of the bathroom. Yes, I am waiting for you. *(Laughs out loud, then resumes)* I am so bored.....They're not going to be here tonight.....Goodman doesn't care......I am so tired of him......Of course, we're going out tonight........I need to do something fun........Surprise, you say?......Oh, surprises? I adore surprises........We're going in your car....Great......Thanks. See you later.

(CHRISTINE enters, drying her hair)

CHRISTINE: Who was on the phone?
KAREN: Nobody important. Don't worry, it wasn't Mark.

(MICHAEL *enters, putting on his shirt)*

MICHAEL: Was that Kayla on the phone?
KAREN: No. The call was for me.
CHRISTINE: Was it Dad?
KAREN: Your Dad doesn't have time for me.
MICHAEL: *(Combing his hair)* Was it Nancy?
KAREN: How do you know?
MICHAEL: I can see it in your eyes. Nancy pays a lot of attention.
KAREN: I've known her since high school. She's my best friend.
CHRISTINE: How come she isn't as successful as you?
KAREN: *(On her way to her room)* She can do what she pleases with her life.
MICHAEL: How come she has no children?
KAREN: *(Closing the door behind her)* She doesn't like to be tied down.
CHRISTINE: I don't like this woman.
MICHAEL: *(To* CHRISTINE*)* We finally agree on something.

(DR. GOODMAN enters. He appears exhausted. He greets his children. They return his greetings)

CHRISTINE: *(To GOODMAN, happily)* I'm so glad I got to see you before I left.

(KAREN enters, looking sharp—hair, clothes, make-up. Addressing GOODMAN)

KAREN: Let's go out tonight. I need it.

DR. GOODMAN: *(Looking at* KAREN *closely)* I see you're all ready to go.

KAREN: That's right. I'm really bored.

DR. GOODMAN: You can go out without me.

KAREN: I knew it, good thing I arranged everything myself.

CHRISTINE: *(Surprised)* You're going out without Dad?

KAREN: Why not?

MICHAEL: *(To his mother)* All by yourself?

KAREN: I know your dad. I'm going out with Nancy.

CHRISTINE: *(To her dad, lovingly)* Do you want me to fix you dinner?

DR. GOODMAN: Did you already eat?

CHRISTINE: Yes. Sorry, Dad. I had to get ready. I'm leaving for Boston tonight.

DR. GOODMAN: And you Michael?

CHRISTINE: *(To her dad)* You know my plane leaves at nine tonight.

KAREN: I don't want to be late. I thought you were going out with me.

DR. GOODMAN: *(At the table, while CHRISTINE prepares his meal)* How do you expect me to go out after working all day at the office?

KAREN: I don't care. It's your responsibility.

DR. GOODMAN: Seems like our married life is taking a different path.

KAREN: That's your opinion.

DR. GOODMAN: We're drifting apart.

KAREN: You no longer enjoy life, it seems like.

DR. GOODMAN: *(Eating)* Are you tired of me?

KAREN: Do you blame me?

DR. GOODMAN: No. I'm just asking.

KAREN: *(Angrily)* You're the one that doesn't listen. You never talk to me.

(She turns away, picks up the remote control, and watches TV. DR. GOODMAN leaves the table, stands, and walks to the other side of the living room. He sits to watch a football game in progress, on another TV set)

MICHAEL: *(Standing in front of his father)*: We waited for you for quite a while.

DR. GOODMAN: You've always waited for me to arrive.

MICHAEL: Today isn't yesterday, Dad!

DR. GOODMAN: *(Sorrily)* I had hoped that sweet life would never cease. Oh, the times when we ate together, played together, talked together, and shared everything.

MICHAEL: Dad, we are in the space age, and things are moving fast.

DR. GOODMAN: Why did you wait for me?

MICHAEL: To say goodbye, and to get my check.

(A car screeches to a halt, CHRISTINE looks out the window, motioning Mark to wait. She hurries toward her father)

CHRISTINE: I must go now, Dad. Can I have the check now?

DR. GOODMAN: Where are you going?

CHRISTINE: Have you forgotten that I start school at Harvard next week?

DR. GOODMAN: And what's going to happen to this family which I worked so hard for?

CHRISTINE: Our family is not going anywhere.

MICHAEL: And you are the one keeping it together.

DR. GOODMAN: How can we be so far away from each other?

CHRISTINE: Father, we're going far. We need to spread out own wings.

MICHAEL: You seem to need us besides you, always.

DR. GOODMAN: What makes you say that?

CHRISTINE: Doesn't our happiness also mean your happiness? *(A car blows its horn)* Dad, please hurry. Mark is waiting, and he's getting nervous.

KAREN: *(In a huff, interrupting, as she gets near them)* Take this check, and go. Seems like your father is trying to humiliate you.

(CHRISTINE takes the check, thanks her mom, bids farewell to her father and brother)

DR. GOODMAN: Your bag, don't forget it. *(She is at the front door with a large bag)* Here, let me help you.

CHRISTINE: Thanks, Dad.

MICHAEL: She can handle her own bags, Dad. She's a big girl.

DR. GOODMAN: She's still my little girl, my baby.

CHRISTINE: Oh thank you, Dad.

(MARK enters)

MARK: *(Apologetic)* We're late, I don't want to miss the plane.

DR. GOODMAN: Then, give her a hand with her luggage.

(MARK and CHRISTINE exit)

MICHAEL: Dad, you're my father, but our lives must evolve. We're no longer children.

DR. GOODMAN: But, but you're still my boy.

MICHAEL: I understand, Dad. But, you seem to not want me to be on my own.

KAREN: He's doing no such thing. We gave you plenty.

MICHAEL: You're counting this against me?

DR. GOODMAN: No. But I must remind you of how much

I've done for you. You don't even have any time for me.

(DR. GOODMAN *takes a few steps back, and stops talking)*

MICHAEL: Oh, Dad, that's ridiculous.
KAREN: Seems like your father doesn't realize that you're becoming a man.
DR. GOODMAN: I might have been negligent toward my family.
KAREN: Now, here is a sensible answer.
DR. GOODMAN: And the children? What are they supposed to give back?
MICHAEL: Seek the future.
DR. GOODMAN: What about honor and respect?
MICHAEL: Dad, you're so old-fashioned.
DR. GOODMAN: Then, you must be self-reliant.
KAREN: Here, take this check and get going, before you miss your flight.
MICHAEL: *(Taking the check and kissing his mother)* Thanks. *(He carries his bag and heads for the door)*
KAREN: Good luck, Son.
MICHAEL: Goodbye, Mom. Goodbye, Dad, and thank you. *(He exits)*
KAREN: *(She walks toward the couch to watch TV)* You must deal with the reality of the situation.
DR. GOODMAN: *(Puzzled)* Situation, what situation? *(As he scans a book)* I think it's Nancy. *(She jumps from her seat, looks out the window, waves)* I'll be right there. *(She faces* DR. GOODMAN*)*Since you don't want to go out with me, I'm going with Nancy.

(She starts to leave)

DR. GOODMAN: *(Visibly upset)* That's right, today is different than yesterday, and I got a strong feeling that tomorrow will be different than today.

CURTAIN

Act Two

Scene 1

SCENE: A night club. Some patrons are eating, drinking, dancing. KAREN and NANCY enter. The host seats them at a table.

KAREN: *(Awkwardly)* I'm afraid my husband won't approve of me being here.
NANCY: You told me that he wouldn't care.
KAREN: That's right, but he might get mad.

(The Waiter appears to take their order. NANCY orders alcoholic beverages)

KAREN: I'm going to forget it all tonight.
NANCY: Good girl, so you can get out of this crisis you're in.

(The Waiter returns with their drinks. NANCY offers one to KAREN)

KAREN: It is true that my husband is becoming boring. *(NANCY laughs out loud)* Why are you laughing?
NANCY: You remind me of my first husband.
KAREN: And how did you handle it?
NANCY: As you know, I married three times, and divorced three times. I decided to stay single.
KAREN: But, but—
NANCY: *(Interrupting)* Don't forget. I am free.
KAREN: It must be hard. Very hard.
NANCY: *(She hands KAREN another drink)* You are a beautiful woman.
KAREN: Unfortunately my husband doesn't think so.
NANCY: *(Whispering, devilishly)* Hey, look at this guy.
KAREN: Why?

NANCY: Look how handsome he is. He sure looks good.
KAREN: Yes, he does look seductive.
NANCY: I know him, and he wants to meet you.
KAREN: Why?
NANCY: He's going through the same thing.
KAREN: You mean he is as lonely as I am?
NANCY: Yes. He's going through a difficult period.
KAREN: Is he married?
NANCY: Yes, but his wife doesn't pay him any attention.
KAREN: I can relate.
NANCY: Like you, he is out to enjoy life and to be fulfilled.

(She hands KAREN another drink)

KAREN: Do you know him well?
NANCY: As much as I know you. *(She touches KAREN's hand)* Let me introduce you. *(NANCY stands and takes KAREN's hand)* Don't be such a chicken, come on.

(KAREN stands and faces the door as though to leave)

NANCY: Please don't. Trust my judgment. All I want is your happiness. I'll help you through this difficult period.
KAREN: It is a difficult time for me.
NANCY: Then, you must have the courage to face it, and do something about it.
KAREN: Something tells me that I must leave.
NANCY: Don't let this opportunity pass you by, please.

(NANCY looks toward a man seated a few feet away. She smiles at him)

NANCY: Joe, Joe.

(JOE *stands, looking tall and handsome. He moves toward them, smiling)*

JOE: Hello.
NANCY: This is my friend Karen.

(KAREN *looks embarrassed)*

JOE: *(To* KAREN) Most delighted to meet you.
KAREN: Thank you.
NANCY: *(Leaving)* Sorry, but I have to go.
KAREN: *(Nervously)* I'll go with you.
NANCY: No, just wait for me. I'll be back shortly to drive you home.
JOE: No need to be afraid. This is a public place.
KAREN: I'm not afraid. I just don't feel right.
JOE: That's because we're not yet acquainted.
KAREN: I have nothing against getting acquainted. Okay.

(She seems more relaxed)

JOE: *(Handing her a drink)* Please. *(She accepts the drink and thanks him)* You really are an attractive woman.
KAREN: You're not bad yourself
JOE: You're fine and sensitive as well.
KAREN: You seem like a gentleman, and I feel more relaxed now, thank you.
JOE: *(Lamenting)* Unfortunately, I'm not happy.
KAREN: *(The alcohol starts to affect her)* Sorry to hear that.
JOE: Please don't be sorry. Seems to me you are in the same predicament.
KAREN: How can you tell?
JOE: I can see it in your eyes.
KAREN: Your eyes say the same thing.

68

JOE: *(Touching her hand, gently)* You are right, my dear. *(He gazes into her eyes)*

KAREN: What do you see in my eyes?

JOE: Just a beautiful feeling, an inner glow.

KAREN: I also am experiencing this inner glow that I can't explain.

JOE: Touching your hand gives me that thing I lost long ago.

KAREN: *(Obviously intoxicated)* I sure miss the romance.

JOE: I also miss that someone with which to share my feelings.

KAREN: And what about your wife?

JOE: Yes, I am married, but not really married.

KAREN: *(Sympathizing)* How similar are we.

JOE: Doesn't your husband appreciate you?

KAREN: He completely ignores me.

JOE: She does me too.

KAREN: Too bad you wife doesn't make you happy.

JOE: She doesn't even try.

KAREN: Why not?

JOE: We live in different worlds.

KAREN: Seems that she never has any time for you.

JOE: Yes, you can say that.

KAREN: Why can't you talk to her about that?

JOE: She really doesn't understand my feelings and my needs.

KAREN: Bet she doesn't know how.

JOE: She won't even let me touch her. She is so cold.

KAREN: You seem like a sensitive and warm human being.

JOE: *(Fondling her hair)* This problem causes me a lot of suffering.

KAREN: I feel for you.

JOE: She even refuses to kiss me or have anything to do with me that way.

KAREN: How can you go on like this?

JOE: I doubt if we'll continue together much longer, especially now, after meeting you.

KAREN: I also don't expect to be with my husband much longer.

JOE: Why is that?

KAREN: He is constantly busy with his patients. Busy at the office, busy researching, busy succeeding and making money—busy, busy all the time.

JOE: And your married life?

KAREN: *(Shapes her thumb and index finger to make a zero)* Zero, zilch. Our life is a mere arrangement. This is no life.

JOE: Seems that your luck is just as bad as mine.

KAREN: I think we might be able to change this together.

JOE: *(He caresses her cheek)* You are as beautiful as life itself.

KAREN: I am life itself

JOE: My wish is to enjoy this life.

KAREN: I need to be fulfilled.

JOE: My desire is to help you find whatever you're looking for.

KAREN: *(Really intoxicated)* You don't know what I need.

(JOE holds her hand, as KAREN stands and attempts to find the door, stumbling. JOE stands. They are holding each other around the waist, heading for the door)

JOE: Let's go to my room at the hotel and see if you can find what you're looking for.

Lights dim and out.

Scene 2

The Scene: DR. GOODMAN's *office. He is reviewing a patient's file. The nurse knocks and enters.*

DR. GOODMAN: I thought you left, what's the matter?

NURSE: I did. But I ran into Joe, and he insisted on meeting with you.

DR. GOODMAN: It's late. The office is supposed to be closed.

NURSE: That's true, doctor. He really insisted on seeing you.

DR. GOODMAN: He can see me tomorrow.

NURSE: He pleaded with me.

DR. GOODMAN: Is he all right?

NURSE: I couldn't tell, but I am puzzled.

DR. GOODMAN: Why is that?

NURSE: Because I have never seen him any happier than he was yesterday.

DR. GOODMAN: Is he still that happy?

NURSE: No. He is depressed.

DR. GOODMAN: Ask him in.

(NURSE exits, JOE enters DR. GOODMAN's *office)*

JOE: Sorry Dr. Goodman for coming without an appointment. I realize it's after nine.

DR. GOODMAN: What happened?

JOE: Yesterday was the happiest day of my life.

DR. GOODMAN: Seems that you found the way out of your depression.

JOE: Not exactly.

DR. GOODMAN: Tell me what happened.

JOE: I was with a woman.

DR. GOODMAN: A woman other than your wife?

JOE: Yes, a stunning woman.

DR. GOODMAN: Did she come on to you or you her?

JOE: A little of both.

DR. GOODMAN: What attracted you to her?

JOE: Her beauty.

DR. GOODMAN: Is she married?

JOE: *(Nodding sorrily)* Yes.

DR. GOODMAN: Did she make that clear from the beginning?

JOE: Yes.

DR. GOODMAN: Does your conscience bother you?

JOE: I couldn't say no to that.

DR. GOODMAN: But you don't have the right to do that.

JOE: Aren't we born to enjoy this life?

DR. GOODMAN: Does your wife know?

JOE: My wife realizes that our life is only an arrangement.

DR. GOODMAN: What do you think she'll do once she finds out that you have betrayed her?

JOE: *(Aggressively)* Don't say betrayal.

GOODMAN: What do you want to call it?

JOE: *(Nervously)* It is a need, yes, a need, a strong need.

GOODMAN: Why not discuss it with your wife, level with her?

JOE: Funny I heard the same question from the beautiful lady.

DR. GOODMAN: And what was your response?

JOE: As I told her, my wife is oblivious to my needs as a husband.

DR. GOODMAN: Then, why not divorce her?

JOE: It is hard to leave her.

DR. GOODMAN: Why?

JOE: Because I need her.

DR. GOODMAN: And why do you need her?

JOE: Because she is a part of my life.

DR. GOODMAN: Do you think your wife is seeing another man?

JOE: Maybe I've been fooled, who knows?

DR. GOODMAN: How would you feel if you learned that she is in fact seeing another man?

JOE: I don't want to know, even if it's true.

DR. GOODMAN: Are your feelings any different now than yesterday?

JOE: Yes.

DR. GOODMAN: How different?

JOE: Yesterday, I was on top of the world. Today, I'm on the bottom.

DR. GOODMAN: Why is that?

JOE: Because I only had a few precious moments with this woman.

DR. GOODMAN: Do you wish to spend the rest of your life with this woman?

JOE: That's hard to say, but I'm sure that I had been fulfilled.

DR. GOODMAN: What about that other woman. What's her story?

JOE: She admitted to total ecstasy while together, the likes of which she has never experienced with her husband.

DR. GOODMAN: Can you live without this woman?

JOE: Without her, I will remain a prisoner of my fate and loneliness.

DR. GOODMAN: Can you divorce your wife?

JOE: Possibly.

DR. GOODMAN: Do you think that woman would be willing to divorce her husband for you?

JOE: I think so?

DR. GOODMAN: What makes you so sure?

JOE: She's unhappy with her husband, and I, with my wife.

DR. GOODMAN: Seems that both of you are selfish in that regard.

JOE: Selfish, yes, possibly.

DR. GOODMAN: My aim is not to blame, but rather, to establish your responsibilities.

JOE: I am living up to my responsibilities, and that's why I feel so guilty.

(The office door opens. KAREN enters. She does not notice JOE as he is seated in a corner not visible from the door)

DR. GOODMAN: Karen, hi.

JOE: *(Not realizing that KAREN is DR. GOOMDAN's wife, in a loud voice)* I can't believe this!

DR. GOODMAN: Can't believe what?

(KAREN looks at JOE. Her mouth opens, and she isn't able to utter a word)

JOE: *(bittersweetly)* This is the beautiful woman I was telling you about.

DR. GOODMAN: *(His face is puzzled, and very much surprised)* Are you sure about that?

JOE: Very sure. *(KAREN faints, and falls to the floor)* Isn't she the prettiest woman in the world? *(JOE is in a confused and clouded state)*

DR. GOODMAN: *(Not wanting to believe the worst)* Are you positive this is the woman you spoke of?

JOE: *(Helping KAREN up)* Yes, I am. She'll tell you what a fool her husband is.

DR. GOODMAN: *(Bitterly)* Indeed, I have been a fool.

JOE: Do you know this lady? *(DR. GOODMAN does not answer. He is visibly shaken up)* Is she one of your patients? *(KAREN comes to)*

KAREN: *(Whispers)* He is my husband.

JOE: *(Overwhelmed by this revelation)* What are you saying?

DR. GOODMAN: That's right. I am her husband, the fool.

JOE: *(Sickened)* I am so sorry. I didn't know. I didn't know she was your wife. Please excuse me *(He heads for the door)* Doctor, I can't bear this.

(JOE exits)

KAREN: I am sorry, I didn't mean to betray you like this.

DR. GOODMAN: *(Teary-eyed, limp with sadness)* Why did you do it?

KAREN: I was so lonely.

DR. GOODMAN: Did this relationship improve your loneliness?

KAREN: I found someone who paid attention to me.

DR. GOODMAN: So you satisfied your desires without any responsibility.

KAREN: I only reacted to my needs.

DR. GOODMAN: Your needs have betrayed and deceived you.

KAREN: I am a woman, full of life.

DR. GOODMAN: But you are my wife. You have responsibilities and duties.

KAREN: It is my duty to be happy, to have a life.

DR. GOODMAN: You have satisfied yourself by stepping on every one in such a selfish way.

KAREN: Who among us isn't selfish?

DR. GOODMAN: Have you forgotten our wedding vows?

KAREN: If the wedding vows don't fulfill you, what good are they?

DR. GOODMAN: Married life is based on mutual understanding, faithfulness, and sacrifice.

KAREN: *(Mockingly)* You still live in an unreal world, in the past, and without regard to one's needs.

DR. GOODMAN: You have really deceived me. You have betrayed my love. I gave you my all, and you abused me. You have betrayed my trust in you. *(Short pause)* My hopes are ruined by what you have done.

KAREN: I am, and feel beautiful.

DR. GOODMAN: You are only looking at the exterior, which causes you to deceive yourself and others. But if you were to look on the inside, you would find ugliness.

KAREN: I made you. You wouldn't have made it without my help and support.

DR. GOODMAN: And you took everything back, by your cheating.

KAREN: I have you more than any other woman can.

DR. GOODMAN: Yes, but only for mere moments.

KAREN: Seems like you're going to lose me.

DR. GOODMAN: Your loss is my gain.

KAREN: What do you mean by that?

DR. GOODMAN: I'm going to divorce you.

KAREN: *(Unmoved and on her way out)* Good, I can use freedom.

DR. GOODMAN: *(As KAREN opens the door)* Yes, I will divorce you, and it hurts me to say it. Go, you cheater. Go, leave me alone.

Lights dim and out

CURTAIN

Act Three

Scene 1

The Scene: The GOODMAN *house. The phone is ringing.* KAREN *enters. She picks up the phone.*

KAREN: Hello. Hi Nancy. Yes, the divorce is final. *(Front door opens. She hesitates)* I think he's here. I'll tell you more when I see you. Bye. *(Puts the phone down.* DR. GOODMAN *walks in. He seems dejected and slow)* Why aren't you in court?

DR. GOODMAN: Why? I'm not being charged with anything.

KAREN: The divorce is final, you know.

DR. GOODMAN: *(Undisturbed)* That's good.

KAREN: I get almost everything, you know.

DR. GOODMAN: You can have everything I have. Here are the car keys, the house keys, the bank books. *(Nervously)* And what else? Oh, the key to my office, here take it.

KAREN: The office? No, you keep this one. You need to work so you can support me.

DR. GOODMAN: *(Laughing nervously)* No, no. this will never happen. I refuse to be your slave.

KAREN: Are you denying me my rights?

DR. GOODMAN: What rights?

KAREN: My rights of half your income.

DR. GOODMAN: Do you think you own me?

KAREN: It's not right for you to close down the office, and deprive your patients of cures.

DR. GOODMAN: Has life been fair to me?

KAREN: You mean me?

DR. GOODMAN: Yes.

KAREN: You forgot that without me you wouldn't be where you are?

DR. GOODMAN: For that, you stabbed me in the back.

KAREN: I gave you everything.

DR. GOODMAN: You gave me, yes. But what you took away is far greater—everything I own.

KAREN: We were partners in everything.

DR. GOODMAN: But you didn't share in my pains, betrayal pains.

KAREN: I have given you my entire life.

DR. GOODMAN: You took my yesterday and my today. But tomorrow isn't yours.

KAREN: Are you angry because you divorced me?

DR. GOODMAN: That's ridiculous.

KAREN: I've never seen you this angry before.

DR. GOODMAN: At least I'm not taking my anger out on you.

KAREN: I'm confident that the revenge thing doesn't exist in you.

DR. GOODMAN: No, my dear. That revenge thing you are referring to, isn't dead in me. But I can control it. And it's the only way to cope with the situation.

KAREN: I'm certain love will get you through.

DR. GOODMAN: Love?

KAREN: Yes, love will remain, even after our divorce.

DR. GOODMAN: Why is that?

KAREN: Because that's what you taught me. Love endures all difficulties.

DR. GOODMAN: I'm not sure about that, at this point.

KAREN: No, no. You were right.

DR. GOODMAN: Why? I don't understand.

KAREN: No need to become enemies. Love for each other is greater than revenge.

DR. GOODMAN: That's good. We need to have peace.

KAREN: You can keep the house.

DR. GOODMAN: No thanks. I don't need anything from you. I don't wish to have anything to do with you, with my office or patients. I am leaving that world behind. I want to be free of everything—no property, no home, no limits—free—free.

KAREN: But the court ordered you to share that freedom with me.

DR. GOODMAN: *(He picks up his suitcase and opens the door)* That's everything I need. I'm getting out with something you can't have.

KAREN: No, no. You will share that with me, whether you like it or not.

DR. GOODMAN: *(Walking out the door)* No, my dear. I will not share myself with anyone.

Lights dim and out.

Scene 2

The Scene: The city slums, along an alley, on a cold and rainy night. A man in his fifties sits huddled around a makeshift fire for warmth. He is sipping on a bottle, while humming a tune. DR. GOODMAN enters. He looks haggard and unkempt. His cough indicates a pulmonary or respiratory infection.

VAGABOND: *(Looks DR. GOODMAN over, without paying much attention)* You sound awful, are you sick?

DR. GOODMAN: Maybe.

VAGABOND: Seems to me you're not used to being homeless.

DR. GOODMAN: I think you're right.

VAGABOND: My name is Richard.

DR. GOODMAN: I'm Dr. Goodman.

VAGABOND: *(Takes a drink, shakes his head)* Goodman. It's been a while since I've met a Good man.

GOODMAN: It's only a name.

VAGABOND: Sit down, get warm *(He offers him a drink)*

DR. GOODMAN: No, thanks, I don't drink.

VAGABOND: Good man, Dr. Goodman.

DR. GOODMAN: Do you always drink?

VAGABOND: You think it's a simple answer?

DR. GOODMAN: Any answer is better than none.

VAGABOND: An answer will take along time, maybe a lifetime.

DR. GOODMAN: Do you drink to keep warm?

VAGABOND: It's going to be a warm night.

DR. GOODMAN: You must be kidding me.

VAGABOND: You're right, but this fire will sure keep us warm.

(The wind howls, causing the fire to be unstable)

DR. GOODMAN: I'm afraid of it.

VAGABOND: I'm an expert on fires. Don't let it worry you.

DR. GOODMAN: Expert, huh? I suppose you're going to put it out with that liquor?

VAGABOND: *(Laughing out loud)* No, no. The liquor only gives me the energy to run away.

DR. GOODMAN: Run away from what?

VAGABOND: From the fire, of course.

DR. GOODMAN: You're drunk.

VAGABOND: No. Not yet.

DR. GOODMAN: I don't know what you mean.

VAGABOND: As I told you, to get way from fire.

DR. GOODMAN: *(Coughing)* I don't understand.

VAGABOND: I worked for the Fire Department.

DR. GOODMAN: You were a fireman?

VAGABOND: Yes.

DR. GOODMAN: And what happened? I'd like to know.

(VAGABOND takes a drink, looks out as if searching for the past)

VAGABOND's voice: It was Christmas Eve, twenty years ago.

The Scene: An ordinary house on Christmas Eve. Caroling, tree trimming, aroma filling the air. A woman in her thirties with young children decorating the house.

CHILD: When will Daddy get home?

MOTHER: I hope soon.

CHILD: Doesn't he know that this is Christmas Eve?

MOTHER: Of course, he does.

CHILD: Maybe he forgot.

MOTHER: No, he didn't forget.

CHILD: Why, then, isn't he here?
MOTHER: He probably got busy.
CHILD: There are no fires on Christmas eve, Mom.
MOTHER: There are fires everyday, son.
CHILD: I'm tired. I want to go to bed.
CHILD 2: Before going to bed, let's write a note to Dad.

(CHILD *hands his sister a pencil and a piece of paper.*)

CHILD 2: *(Reading as she writes)* We waited a long time. We hope you arrive before Santa Claus.

(They hang the note on the tree. The mother and her children are singing carols, on their way to bed.)

VAGABOND's voice: They left the Christmas tree lights on, how neat!
DR. GOODMAN's voice: *(Coughing)* What a great idea.
VAGABOND's voice: With plenty of presents at its foot.
DR. GOODMAN's voice: Seems like a terrific evening.
VAGABOND's voice: *(Sobbing)* Unforgettable.

(The clock shows two a.m. VAGABOND enters drunk, and exhausted. He admires the tree. He reads the note and tosses it under the Christmas tree. An electrical spark ignites the note, and a fire starts. He is astonished and overwhelmed.)

The Scene: Return to VAGABOND *and* DR. GOODMAN *by their makeshift fire.*

DR. GOODMAN: Where did you go that night?
VAGABOND: *(Broken speech)* Went to the bar with a friend.
DR. GOODMAN: You went and got drunk on Christmas Eve?

VAGABOND: It hurts so much.

DR. GOODMAN: Your family was waiting for you.

VAGABOND: Yes, they waited for a long time.

DR. GOODMAN: Did you put the fire out?

VAGABOND: I thought I was dreaming the whole thing. I thought the liquor made me see things.

DR. GOODMAN: What happened next?

VAGABOND: The tree burned down, along with the presents. The house burned down. I ran to save myself, not thinking, not thinking about my family asleep in the house.

DR. GOODMAN: You made no attempt to save your family?

VAGABOND: I watched the whole thing burn in my drunken stupor. Some fireman I am!

DR. GOODMAN: *(Coughing and wheezing uncontrollably)* Then what did you do?

VAGABOND: I had a morbid fear of living in houses after my house burned down. I can't even be around people, after I lost my family. It's been twenty years now.

DR. GOODMAN: These are truly painful memories.

VAGABOND What about you? How long have you been a homeless person?

DR. GOODMAN: *(Coughing)* Only a few months.

VAGABOND: That sounds really bad.

DR. GOODMAN: I don't care.

VAGABOND: What did you do before?

DR. GOODMAN: A psychiatrist.

VAGABOND: And now you are the patient.

DR. GOODMAN: Who says?

VAGABOND: Society, that's who.

DR. GOODMAN: We are its victims.

VAGABOND: We are life's victims.

DR. GOODMAN: Yes, life and my wife.

VAGABOND: Was your wife your life?

DR. GOODMAN: She owned me. All along I thought I was in control.

VAGABOND: *(Mockingly)* I think this cold weather has affected your lungs and your brains.

DR. GOODMAN: Maybe my lungs. But I see things much clearer since I left her.

VAGABOND: Can't you cure yourself?

DR. GOODMAN: My cure is being away from her.

VAGABOND: You really loved her, didn't you?

DR. GOODMAN: I trusted her completely.

VAGABOND: Were you faithful?

DR. GOODMAN: Absolutely.

VAGABOND: Why then did she go out on you?

DR. GOODMAN: *(Coughing profusely)* God only knows.

VAGABOND: Do you want to start over?

DR. GOODMAN: Yes, but differently.

VAGABOND: You are a good man, Dr. Goodman. *(VAGABOND shivers, coughs deeply)* It's really cold tonight.

DR. GOODMAN: *(Putting his jacket on VAGABOND)* Here, put this on.

VAGABOND: Why are you doing this?

DR. GOODMAN: Because you're shivering, man.

VAGABOND: What about you?

DR. GOODMAN: It's okay, I'm warm on the inside.

VAGABOND: Haven't eaten in two days. I'm hungry.

(DR. GOODMAN takes a part of a sandwich and hands it to VAGABOND)

VAGABOND: Why are you giving me your food?

DR. GOODMAN: I don't need it. I can get over hunger.

VAGABOND: You are hurting.

DR. GOODMAN: It's only temporary *(He coughs painfully)*

VAGABOND: Let me get you some help, the paramedics.

DR. GOODMAN: Don't worry, friend. I have an inner peace which allows me to break my chains and to be free of worry and rid myself of worldly worries and pain.

(DR. GOODMAN stumbles and falls off stage. He is going toward the front door, dragging himself. He stumbles, falls, stands, and finally drops motionless at the front door of the theater)

VAGABOND: Pity, this is the end of Dr. Goodman, the Good Man. I feel so bad. I could have done more for him, if it hadn't been for this liquor. Goodman's gone. His wife doesn't know how much he needed her. His children, his patients, and every one who knew him, don't know how much he needed them. They didn't know how to hold on to him.

VAGABOND: *(In a loud voice)* Goodman, let me get you to the hospital. No forget it.

(Enter CHRISTINE and MICHAEL)

CHRISTINE *(To VAGABOND)*: Where did he go?
VAGABOND: Are you also looking for Goodman?
CHRISTINE: Yes, he's my father.
VAGABOND: I'm afraid you're too late.
CHRISTINE: What do you mean?
VAGABOND: He fell. He collapsed.
MICHAEL: Collapsed?
VAGABOND: Yeah, that's life.
CHRISTINE: Are you drunk?
VAGABOND: Maybe. But I've discovered the truth.
MICHAEL: Truth?
VAGABOND: Yeah. The world took everything from him, and he took nothing.
CHRISTINE: Please tell us where he is.

VAGABOND: He collapsed. He collapsed from his pain, from his sickness, and from his loneliness and suffering.
MICHAEL: Where? Where did he collapse?
VAGABOND: In the middle of the crowd.
CHRISTINE: Where? We've got to help him.
VAGABOND: You're too late. If you look for him, you won't find him. You might hear his voice. No, no, no, his voice. You'll hear his cries and moans.

(He cries out for DR. GOODMAN. *With* CHRISTINE *and* MICHAEL, *he steps off the stage, and they follow the crowd toward the exit/front door chanting "GOODMAN....GOODMAN")*